Men-at-Arms • 7

The Black Brunswickers

Otto von Pivka • Illustrated by Michael Roffe

First published in Great Britain in 1973 by Osprey Publishing,
PO Box 883, Oxford, OX1 9PL, UK
PO Box 3985, New York, NY 10185-3985, USA
Email: info@ospreypublishing.com

Osprey Publishing, part of Bloomsbury Publishing Plc

Transferred to digital print on demand 2016.

First published 1973.
3rd impression 2005.

Printed and bound by PrintOnDemand-Worldwide.com, Peterborough, UK.

A CIP catalogue record for this book is available from the British Library.

ISBN: 978 0 85045 146 7

Series Editor: Martin Windrow

Acknowledgements

I wish to acknowledge the invaluable assistance given to me in the preparation of this
book by the authorities and staff of the Landesmesuem in Brunswick, the members of the
Berlin section of the Gesellschaft für Heereskunde, and my many friends and comrades in
that city.

The Woodland Trust

Osprey Publishing is supporting the Woodland Trust, the UK's leading woodland
conservation charity, by funding the dedication of trees.

www.ospreypublishing.com

Before we can delve into the details of the uniforms, campaigns and organization of the troops of the Duchy of Braunschweig-Luneburg-Oels it is necessary to cast a brief look at the political situation in Europe during the Napoleonic era in order to see why it was that these Germans, with no direct connection to the British crown, entered its service and fought so bravely against Napoleon.

Before 1870, Germany, as a cohesive state, such as there was in 1914, did not exist. Instead, the area which is now occupied by the two Germanies (the Federal Republic of Germany in the West and the German Democratic Republic in the East), and part of what is nowadays termed Poland, was a raggle-taggle collection of electorates, duchies, grand duchies, principalities and kingdoms. These states, mostly small, were politically divided among themselves, mutually fearful, if not sometimes openly hostile, and, for the most part, without any influence on affairs outside their own, very limited, borders. Together with Austria they formed the Holy Roman Empire and some of the rulers had the right to cast a vote in the election of the emperor. Traditionally, the emperor was the Austrian head of state but there had been exceptions to this: for instance, from 1742 to 1745, when the Elector Karl Albrecht of Bavaria had occupied the Imperial throne because the Austrian head of state was then a woman, Queen Maria Theresa.

Apart from voting for the emperor, each state was required to provide a *Kontingent* of troops when needed by the emperor for use against the enemies of the Empire. This delightfully democratic Imperial military system had obvious disadvantages, however, particularly when one considers all the various and different drill regulations which were used and the fact that practically every state produced its own firearms, each to its own calibre and specifications. In short, the Holy Roman Empire, as it existed in 1796 when Napoleon burst on to the European military and political scene in a blaze of energy and decision, was a colourful but totally outmoded and semi-fossilized institution.[1]

The Imperial Army managed to stay on the battlefield against the Revolutionary French forces until 1800, but constant bickering among its commanders and the old-fashioned system of tactics ensured that its days were numbered, and finally, at the battle of Hohenlinden in Bavaria on 3 December 1800, the military power of the Holy Roman Empire was shattered, leaving only the gaudy titles on the European stage; and these, too, were to vanish in 1805.

In 1805 Napoleon, who was then in firm, and popular, dictatorial command of the French nation and army, was about to extend his grip

The Duke of Brunswick

3

George III (National Army Museum)

Britain's main contribution to these early Coalition Wars against France in Europe was limited to two fields: money and intelligence. British gold paid for the muskets and ammunition of Austrian, Prussian and Russian soldiers, and British agents intrigued against France and sought to stiffen their wavering allies.

In 1803 Napoleon had overrun the Electorate of Hanover thus deepening the rift between France and England, whose monarch (George III) was, of course, also the Elector of Hanover. Most of the Hanoverian Army made its way to England where they became the King's German Legion.

Until 1805 an uneasy peace reigned in Europe, but the same year the restless French Emperor was again opposed by yet another unsteady coalition (the Third Coalition). On this occasion Austria and Russia entered the lists against him, backed by British gold and the hope that Prussia and Saxony would help them with more tangible means. King Frederick William III of Prussia, a weak and vacillating monarch, dithered on the side-lines until it was too late to achieve anything, his procrastination contributing largely to the Austro-Russian defeats in this campaign.

On 17 October 1805 the Austrian commander in Germany, Feldmarschall-Leutnant Mack, was surrounded and forced to capitulate at Ulm with 20,000 men.[2] Mack had pushed far into hostile Bavarian territory at the start of the campaign and was waiting in Ulm to be joined by a strong Russian force when Napoleon, moving with characteristic speed and outnumbering Mack's troops by three to one, encircled him, forcing a humiliating surrender. The majority of Napoleon's forward troops in this operation were Germans – Bavarians, Württembergers and Badenese – and his victory was aided by some incredibly bad liaison work on the part of his Austrian and Russian foes.[3] (At this time Napoleon had just abandoned his scheme to invade England, but his naval strategy was dealt a heavy blow on 21 October 1805 when Nelson destroyed the French and Spanish fleets at Trafalgar.) The Russians and Austrians were not yet in the mood to surrender, however, and another crushing defeat was needed, that of Austerlitz on 2 December 1805, to force them to come to terms with him.

In the subsequent Treaty of Pressburg, on

on the mainland of Europe. It was the era of the Coalition Wars in which Revolutionary France was opposed by a rapidly changing kaleidoscope of European monarchies, whom she repeatedly defeated or who defeated themselves by dissolving into mutually isolated, hostile, self-seeking sub-groups. Prussia and Austria squabbled over Silesia; Saxony feared annexation from Prussia; Prussia looked nervously at Russia over her newly acquired Polish provinces, and England, although the greatest naval power in the world at that time, did not possess a large enough army both to enter the lists on the European mainland and to maintain her colonial possessions against French and Dutch opposition.

Added to this martial weakness on land was the fact that Napoleon already controlled most of the European coastline facing England and thus any attempt at intervention on the Continent would have to have been opened with an opposed landing on a hostile coast, a task for which the British Government (and the Army) had little enthusiasm.

26 December 1805, the Holy Roman Empire was officially dissolved and Emperor Franz II, having already renounced his electoral title, became known simply as Emperor Franz I of Austria. Titles were not the only thing which the Austrian monarch lost however: the Tyrol and the Inn provinces were given to Bavaria, and Vorarlberg to Württemberg. Both these states then became kingdoms and Baden, which had also increased in size at Austria's expense, became a grand duchy.

As a lesson to Prussia for her side-line dithering, Napoleon took from her the principalities of Cleve and Neuchâtel. Cleve he united with the former Bavarian Duchy of Berg to make the Duchy of Cleve-Berg which he then granted to Murat, his flamboyant cavalry commander. Neuchâtel went to Berthier, his chief of staff, and as compensation for these territorial losses, Prussia was given Hanover. This state of affairs was not to continue, however. By 1806 Napoleon, seeking an agreement with England over seaborne trade

Lancer, Cleve-Berg Regiment

with Europe, was offering Hanover back to George III, without bothering too much about the protests raised by the Prussian King. Frederick William III of Prussia was incensed at being so handled and, in a rare moment of decision, declared war on France. Saxony and Brunswick joined Prussia and both sides marshalled their forces.

Inevitably, Austria and Russia could not be brought to concert their efforts with Prussia against France, and thus Napoleon was presented with yet another splendid opportunity to defeat his enemies in detail. Gathering his German 'allies' up as he advanced, he rushed through southern Germany with a force made up of troops from France, Baden, Württemberg, Bavaria, Frankfurt, Hesse-Darmstadt and Würzburg. He caught the Prussian-Saxon-Brunswick Army unprepared and smashed them at the twin battles of Jena and Auerstadt on 14 October 1806. Duke Karl Wilhelm Ferdinand, the then Duke of Brunswick, was a field-marshal in the Prussian Army at the battle and was wounded in action, dying shortly afterwards.

As a result of this 'French' victory, Saxony was

Frederick William III of Prussia

Hussar trooper of the Black Horde in 1809 wearing the long off-white greatcoat with wrist-length cape. Colours of the rest of the uniform are given in the Colour Plates

forced to break her alliance with Prussia and to join the French-controlled Confederation of the Rhine; the Prussian Army disintegrated, the remnants fleeing eastwards.

By now Russia had decided to join Prussia in defying Napoleon, but in turn their joint armies were defeated at Friedland on 14 June 1807. The subsequent Treaty of Tilsit (7 July 1807), signed on a raft moored in the middle of the river Niemen, gave Napoleon yet another opportunity to demonstrate his skill as an inventive European cartographer. Brunswick was dissolved as a state, its former territories being incorporated into the new Napoleonic kingdom of Westphalia, which also included parts of the old states of Hanover and Hesse-Kassel.

Prussia lost much land which went to set up the Grand Duchy of Warsaw, and Saxony gained some territory at Prussia's expense and was elevated from an electorate to a kingdom, joining the Confederation of the Rhine at the same time. The King of Saxony was also created Grand Duke of Warsaw, but Warsaw was an independent member of the Confederation of the Rhine and the Saxon King's secondary title was indeed hollow!

Europe lapsed once more into an uneasy peace. It is against this violent and turbulent background that we begin our detailed study of the Black Brunswickers.

The Formation of the Black Horde

When the Duchy of Brunswick was dissolved in 1807 the son of the dead duke, the dispossessed Friedrich Wilhelm, fled to Austrian territory to nurture in exile his hatred of the French dictator.

Peace again reigned on the European mainland until 1808, but then the war in the Spanish peninsula broke out with the rejection by proud Spaniards of their new king, Joseph Bonaparte – Napoleon's brother – whom the Corsican had attempted to force down their throats.

Since the bitter defeats and loss of territory of 1805, Austria had been hard at work overhauling and expanding her military machine. Although much had been accomplished in this field, Archduke Charles, brother of Emperor Franz I and the man in overall charge of these army reforms, was not convinced that the Austrian forces were yet in a state to be matched against the French Army. His protests were overridden, however, as the Austrian Government felt that with the eruption of the Spanish war, Napoleon would be too occupied to be able to devote large forces to deal with them. Apart from the regular Austrian forces, extensive *Landwehr* (militia) formations had been raised, equipped, armed and semi-trained; a number of volunteer corps were also raised.

6

On 25 February 1809 Friedrich Wilhelm of Brunswick entered into an agreement with the Austrians to raise a corps of infantry and cavalry to fight alongside them as they invaded his old domains, raising the population against their French rulers. Initially, this corps was to consist of an infantry regiment and a hussar regiment each of 1,000 men. The infantry regiment was organized in two battalions each of four companies and the hussar regiment had eight squadrons. The hussar regiment had a horse artillery battery attached to it consisting of two light 7-pounder howitzers and two light 6-pounder cannon.

To set the new corps on its feet the Austrian Government provided the following items:

1,000 infantry shakos
1,000 hussar shakos
1,000 pairs of shoes
1,000 pairs of hussar boots (*Czismen*)
1,000 pairs of spurs
1,000 hussar-pattern waistbelts
1,000 cavalry cartridge pouches
1,000 infantry cartridge pouches
1,000 infantry overcoats
1,000 sets of hussar-pattern harness
1,000 carbines
1,000 infantry muskets with slings
1,000 brace of pistols
The cloth (pepper-and-salt mixture) for 1,000 cavalry greatcoats
2 light 7-pounder howitzers with all accessories
2 light 6-pounder cannon with all accessories
8 ammunition waggons and 240 rounds for each gun, together with the necessary case-shot cartridges
240 rounds of ammunition per head for each infantry-man and cavalryman
12,000 musket flints
12,000 pistol flints
25 *Windbüchsen* (This was a repeating air rifle capable of firing 12 rounds at an effective range of about 200 paces, almost noiselessly, before requiring a recharged air cylinder. For its era it was a very advanced weapon, invented by Girardoni but it required skilful maintenance and after Girardoni's death it fell into disuse.)

The town of Nachod in Bohemia was selected as the forming-up place for the Brunswick Corps and on 1 April 1809 both the infantry and cavalry regiments assembled for the first time.

Horse artillery battery gunner, 1809. Other ranks wore infantry shakos. The coat is a short *Kollet* in black with six rows of black lace on the chest and three rows of black glass buttons. Collar, shoulder-straps, Polish cuffs and skirt turnbacks are light-blue, as are the narrow trouser stripes. Leatherwork is black with brass furniture, and the brass-hilted sabre has a steel scabbard. Officers wore infantry officers' shakos with hussar officers' *Polrock* coats. Sashes, legwear and equipment were as for hussar officers, the black bandolier bearing a gold, heart-shaped shield with the ducal cipher *FW*. Horse furniture was hussar pattern, and guns and limbers were painted grey

The dispossessed Friedrich Wilhelm of Brunswick was totally concerned with the idea of revenge against Napoleon for the damage which had been done to his family and lands. As a physical expression of this vengeance he decided to clothe his new troops all in black and adopted as his badge the skull and crossbones. As a result he became known as *Der Schwarzer Herzog* (the Black Duke) and his corps was christened *Die Schwarze Schar* (the Black Horde).

The Campaign of 1809

Since the humiliating defeat of 1805 Austria had been licking her wounds and waiting for an opportunity to take revenge. The revolt of the Spanish people against their newly appointed king, Joseph Bonaparte, had caused Napoleon to enter that country to prop up his brother's sagging throne, and Austria judged the time right to strike at the French even though Archduke Charles, who had been entrusted with military reforms after 1805, warned the War Council that the Landwehr was not yet ready for general combat.

By the terms of the Peace of Pressburg (26 December 1805) Austria had lost the Tyrol to Bavaria and now fomented discontent among the Tyroleans who were to rise against the Bavarian occupation forces and eject them from their mountain province. Apart from the Tyrol Austria had lost many Italian Illyrian and Dalmatian lands and was ringed with enemies. Russia was not in any fit state to enter the lists on Austria's side and Prussia, still stunned by the dreadful collapse of her army in 1806, was most unco-operative and almost hostile. England provided plenty of financial aid, but her only armed intervention was in Portugal.

The rest of the German states were now safely welded to the side of France in the Confederation of the Rhine, and even if they secretly wished to help Austria, they were totally unable to demonstrate their loyalties. Napoleon, well informed of Austria's military preparations, ordered her to disarm, but in April 1809 Austria opened hostilities at four points.

Archduke Ferdinand d'Este was ordered to invade Poland and initially met with easy success and entered Warsaw with 36,000 men. He was opposed by a 14,000-strong Saxon-Polish force under Prince Poniatowski; the main armies of Saxony and Poland were employed in Austria and Spain.

After the battle of Raszyn on 19 April 1809, the Saxon contingent of Poniatowski's force (two and a half battalions of infantry) were recalled to Saxony. In Saxony itself, Oberst Thielmann had been placed in command of a force put together from various depot troops which later grew to eight battalions of infantry, each of 1,000 men and a half a battalion of the Leib-grenadiergarde.

These troops opposed the Austrian force under Generalmajor am Ende which was in and around Theresienstadt in Bohemia. Part of this force was the Duke of Brunswick's Black Horde and the

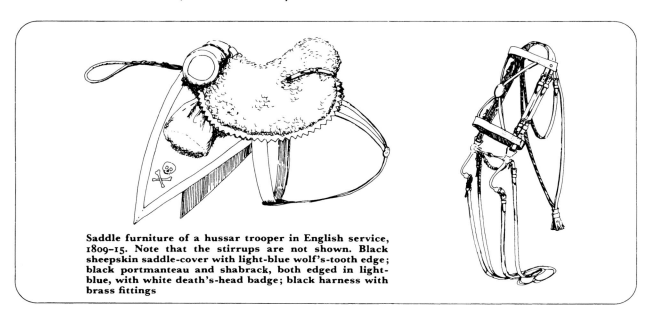

Saddle furniture of a hussar trooper in English service, 1809–15. Note that the stirrups are not shown. Black sheepskin saddle-cover with light-blue wolf's-tooth edge; black portmanteau and shabrack, both edged in light-blue, with white death's-head badge; black harness with brass fittings

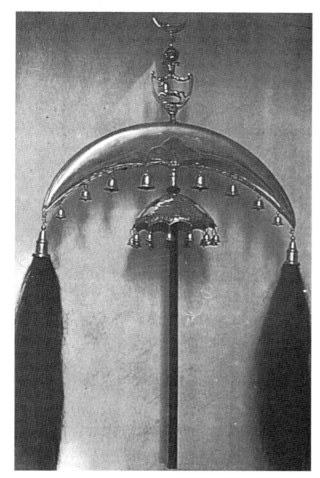

Landwehr, Brunswickers and Hessians) and ordered him to make a diversionary raid into Saxony. On 10 June this raid began and the Duke of Brunswick moved his corps out of the town of Aussig.

Thielmann, whose forces had brushed with the Brunswickers already, evacuated Dresden and moved all his forces to Gorbitz, and the next day, 11 June, the combined force of General am Ende occupied Dresden. On 12 June the Brunswickers and some Austrian Jägers advanced on Gorbitz and pushed Thielmann and the Saxons back, via Pennrich, Wilsdruff and Birkenhain, to Nessen. Ten Saxons were killed and forty-seven were wounded.

The King of Saxony had appealed to King Jerome of Westphalia, another of Napoleon's brothers, to come to his aid, and a sizable force of French, Dutch, Westphalian and Bergisch troops was assembled. But due to the activities of the Prussian Major von Schill who, with his regiment, the 2nd (Brandenburg) Hussars, had broken out of his garrison at Potsdam without the approval or knowledge of his king, and was

The First Battalion of the Black Horde had a band and in 1809 Queen Charlotte Sophia of England presented Duke Friedrich Wilhelm with this _Schellenbaum_ or 'Jingling Johnnie' to be carried at the head of the band. It is now in the Brunswick Landesmuseum. (It was presented by the officers of the Brunswicker 92nd Infantry Regiment who had inherited it and carried it until 1918.) Unique in having down-turned horns rather than up-swept, it originally had red horse-tails, but these were replaced by the black ones illustrated. The Black Horde had no flags or standards until 1815

Kurhessischen Korps of the deposed Prince of Hesse-Kassel. The Austrian forces in Bohemia remained on the defensive and did not invade Saxony until after a certain amount of provocation on the part of the Saxons under Oberst Thielmann.

Encouraged by his opponents' lack of activity, Thielmann invaded Bohemia on 25 May 1809, while on 30 and 31 May the Black Horde stormed and captured the Saxon town of Zittau. Thielmann then withdrew to Dresden.

After the battle of Aspern Esslingen (21/22 May 1809), Archduke Charles of Austria reinforced General am Ende's force to 10,000 men (Line,

Guards of King Jerome's Westphalian Regiment

rampaging his way through the old Prussian provinces of Westphalia, Jerome was very slow to concentrate his forces and come to the aid of the Saxon King.

On 24 June Jerome's force consisted of:

X Corps of the 1st German Army
1st Westphalian Guards Division
Commander – Divisionsgeneral Graf Bernterode

One squadron Garde du Corps	140 men
One battalion Grenadiergarde	840 men
One battalion Jägergarde	600 men
Three squadrons Chevaulegersgarde	550 men
One battalion Jäger-Carabiniers	360 men
	2,490 men

Dolman and waistcoat of a subaltern officer of the Lieb-Bataillon, 1815. Note the narrow shoulders and embroidery in black on the blue collar of the dolman, and in silver on the blue collar of the waistcoat. The waistcoat buttons are plain silver spheres, and those of the dolman are covered with black cloth. Note also the black embroidery above the pointed cuffs

2nd Westphalian Division
Commander – Divisionsgeneral D'Albignac

1st Westphalian Line Infantry Regiment	1,680 men
5th Westphalian Line Infantry Regiment	1,800 men
6th Westphalian Line Infantry Regiment	1,700 men
1st Westphalian Kürassier Regiment	260 men
	5,440 men

3rd Dutch Division
Commander – Divisionsgeneral Gration

6th Dutch Line Infantry Regiment
7th Dutch Line Infantry Regiment
8th Dutch Line Infantry Regiment
9th Dutch Line Infantry Regiment
2nd Dutch Kürassier Regiment
Three companies of artillery

a total of 5,300 men

Also in Westphalia were the following forces:

Commander – Oberst Chabert
3rd Bergisch Line Infantry Regiment – 1,000 men in Kassel
28th French Light Infantry Regiment ⎫ 3,000 men
22nd French Line Infantry Regiment ⎪ in all,
27th French Line Infantry Regiment ⎬ partly in
30th French Line Infantry Regiment ⎪ Homburg and
33rd French Line Infantry Regiment ⎪ partly in
65th French Line Infantry Regiment ⎭ Magdeburg

In addition to these mobile forces, there were 2,300 Mecklenburgers and 800 Oldenburgers as garrisons in the fortresses along the Oder as follows:

Stettin	400 men under Brigadegeneral Libert
Stralsund	1,100 men under Brigadegeneral Candras
Küstrin	2,000 men (commander unknown)

Thielmann's Saxon Corps of about 2,000 men consisted of:

Four squadrons of Kürassiers (von Zastrow)
One squadron of Chevaulegers (von Polenz)
Three squadrons of Saxon Hussars
The Grenadier-Bataillon (von Einsiedel)
One combined infantry battalion (Wolan)
Two companies of infantry regiment (von Burgsdorf)
One musketeer battalion of infantry regiment (von Oebschelwitz)
Two and a half foot artillery batteries
One horse artillery battery

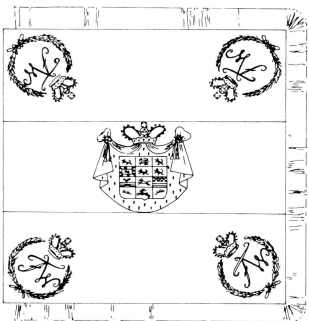

Herzogs Fahne (Duke's Flag), 1st Line Battalion, 1815. On 14 March the ladies of Brunswick presented the Black Duke with six embroidered flags which were transferred to the three line battalions the following month. That of the 1st Battalion was later carried by the 1st Battalion 92nd Infantry Regiment. The central cross is light-blue, the corners yellow, and all charges are silver. There is a silver fringe

Herzogs Fahne (reverse). There are three equal horizontal stripes of yellow, light-blue and yellow, with silver charges in the corners and the ducal arms in the centre

Jerome sent part of his Guards Division and the 3rd Bergisch Infantry Regiment to Eisenach, to reinforce the Saxon King's Personal Guard, and on 18 June 1809 he left Kassel with the rest of the Guards Division, the 2nd Westphalian Division and the 3rd Dutch Division, crossed the river Saale and on 25 June entered Merseburg.

Meanwhile, the Austrians and Brunswickers had occupied Leipzig on 22 June (where the Gelernte Jägers were raised), but on the approach of Jerome's superior forces they left the city again on 24 June. Jerome entered the city amid pealing church bells and much public jubilation on 26 June.

On 28 June the 2nd Westphalian Division had a brush with the Brunswickers.

The Austrian forces in the area were now formed into the XI Corps under Feldmarschall-Leutnant Freiherr von Kienmayer and the main weight of their offensive was transferred south into Franconia. By dint of skilful use of mobility, the Austrian-Brunswick forces avoided battle with their enemies and kept them off balance. Leaving a 'bait' of some Landwehr battalions on the road

to Dresden, the Austro-Brunswick main force slipped off south. On 1 July 1809 Jerome entered Dresden, but his foes had long since gone. He sent General von Bongars in pursuit, but von Bongars followed a cold trail to Halle in Saxony. Until 4 July Jerome stayed in Dresden and then moved off south to Hof where he hoped to join up with Junot's Corps which was already in Franconia.

Kienmayer and the Austrians had been pushed out of Nürnberg by Junot with 10,000 men and fell back towards Hof and took the offensive against Junot on 8 July at Berneck and Gefraess. Having halted the French, Kienmayer turned on Jerome and confronted him at Hof on 11 July after having spent two days in Bayreuth.

Jerome, who was at Plauen, then fell back to Schleiz, Kienmayer followed and confronted him there again on 13 July. After a few cannon shots Jerome fell back to Neustadt an der Orla where there was another skirmish. On 15 July Jerome fell back again to Erfurt which he reached on 17 July. The withdrawal was more of a rout and Jerome's effort to join up with Junot had ended in near-disaster.

In Erfurt Jerome heard that an armistice had been signed between France and Austria and, without waiting to ensure that Saxony no longer required the aid she had initially requested, he thankfully hurried back to Kassel, his capital, with 2,000 men of the Guards Division, his Kürassier Regiment, the 1st and 6th Westphalian Line Infantry Regiments and the 3rd Bergisch Infantry Regiment. Gratien's 3rd Dutch Division remained in Erfurt and Thielmann's Saxons remained in Saxony.

The armistice had been signed at Znaim on 12 July 1809 and Kienmayer's Austrians ceased fighting. The Black Duke, however, did not consider himself in any way bound by this armistice; in fact, it left him in a hopeless position. He therefore decided to fight his way out to the north German coast where he hoped to be able to get his force to England on British warships. Most of his corps seemed quite happy at this prospect of self-imposed exile in a foreign land, but a small section of his officers requested termination of their commissions and attempted to spread disaffection among the loyal men.

The fight to the Coast

The Black Duke parted from the Austrians and on 26 July (after the 3rd Infantry Battalion had been formed and the Uhlans had joined the Hussars at Zwickau) he entered Halle (in the kingdom of Westphalia), emptied the public chests, recruited new men and pulled down the Westphalian crest. The next day Jerome ordered General Rewbell in Hanover, General Gratien in Erfurt and General Michaud in Magdeburg, to close in on the duke and destroy him.

Rewbell collected together in Celle the 1st and 6th Westphalian Line Infantry Regiments, the 1st Westphalian Kürassier Regiment, the 3rd Bergisch Line Infantry Regiment and ten guns, and ordered the 5th Westphalian Infantry Regiment to join him. This latter unit was in Halberstadt on 29 July and was 3,000 men strong.

The Black Duke heard that they were in an exposed position in the town and resolved to attack them.

At this time, his forces consisted of:

Infantry (Commander – Oberst von Bernewitz)

1st Battalion	500 men under Major von Fragstein
2nd Battalion	500 men under Major von Reichmeister
3rd Battalion	150 men under Major von Herzberg
Scharfschützen	150 men under Major von Scriever

Cavalry

Hussars	550 men, the regiment was commanded by Major Schrader as the Oberstleutnant, von Steinmann, was recovering from a wound
Uhlanen	80 men under Rittmeister Graf von Wedell

Artillery (Premier-Leutnant Genderer)

4 guns	80 men
	Total: 100 officers and 2,010 men

The 5th Westphalian Infantry Regiment got news of the approach of the Black Horde and set about putting Halberstadt, an old walled town, into a good state of defence. At 6 p.m. on 29 July the Brunswickers arrived outside the walls of the town and the Westphalian commanding officer, Oberst Graf Wellingerode, sent out a few companies of his regiment to throw them back. A few rounds of canister from the duke's artillery sent them scuttling back into the town and the gates were hurriedly shut and barred. Surrounding the town with patrols, the duke assembled assault columns and led one of them against the Harsleber Gate. A second column assaulted the Kuhlinger Gate. Here the fighting was heavy and casualties numerous until the gates were shot in by a gun crewed by officers. The Brunswick Scharfschützen then rushed in, pulled away some carts full of manure which blocked the road behind the gate, and the Brunswickers poured into the town shouting 'Sieg oder Tod!' (Victory or death).

The fight at the Harsleber Gate had also cost the lives of many of the Black Horde before a Leutnant von Hertell, of the 2nd Infantry Battalion, succeeded in setting fire to the wooden obstructions in the gateway. Two companies of the 2nd Battalion managed to cut down the postern gate of the Johannis Gate and also gained entrance to the town.

The Cavalry of the Black Horde entered the town by the Kuhlinger Gate and rushed through the town until they came upon the enemy reserve of several hundred men in the main square. It was dark and the reserve thought that they were

Subaltern of the Leib-Bataillon in undress uniform, 1815. The black cap has a light-blue headband; the collars of the dolman and waistcoat and the wide trouser stripes are also light-blue. Dolman lace and buttons are black, waistcoat lace and buttons are silver. The gloves are dark-green, the sabre-strap silver and gold

confronted by superior forces and when challenged to throw down their weapons and surrender did so. There was a period of house-to-house fighting, the Westphalian commander was captured by a bold officer of the Black Hussars, as was the commandant of the town, Platzmajor Stockmayer, and gradually the fighting died

down. Only a few hundred Westphalians held out in a big house near the Breiten Gate until dawn.

Next day the Brunswickers found that they had captured 80 officers and 2,000 men and that the Westphalian dead and wounded numbered about 600. Among the dead were about twenty Westphalian gendarmes who were hated by the Brunswickers. The flags of the 5th Westphalian Infantry Regiment were also taken, but what happened to them is a mystery. About one hundred Westphalians escaped.

The Brunswickers' losses were 400 killed and wounded. After replenishing his ammunition and equipment from captured stocks, and recruiting over 300 men from the Westphalian soldiers, the Black Duke pushed on to his old capital of Brunswick which he reached on the evening of 31 July. On 1 August he fought his way through a Westphalian and Bergisch force at Oelper under General Rewbell. There was no general uprising in the duke's favour, probably because the hoped-for English invasion in north Germany had not occurred and only a few gunboats had in fact appeared.

After the skirmish at Oelper, Rewbell pulled off north towards Celle and then re-advanced on Oelper to find that the Black Duke had gone towards Hanover, and on 4 August he reached Hoya. Rewbell followed slowly via Burghorf, crossed the river Leine and later continued northwest to Hoya on the Weser. Rewbell had no certain information concerning the duke's movements and did not seem too keen to catch him and in any case the bridge over the Weser had been destroyed by the duke's men which further slowed the pursuit.

The Black Duke went on to Delmenhorst, but left a weak rearguard behind with instructions to withdraw north towards Bremen and thus lead the enemy away from his real embarkation point which was Elsfleth on the west side of the Weser. The ruse succeeded and after a skirmish at Heidrug the rearguard were able to rejoin the main body at Elsfleth on 6 August, leaving Rewbell slowly marching and counter-marching, trying to decide which trail to follow. The Black Horde (now 1,600 men strong) even had time to sell off their horses before embarking on English ships which took them first to Heligoland and thence to the Isle of Wight, where they went into a period of reorganization before entering British service and fighting in the Peninsula.

King Jerome was furious with Rewbell, who previously had been his favourite, and sent General von Bongars to Bremen on 10 August with orders to remove Rewbell from his position of command. Rewbell, however, was not to be found; sensing that things might be getting unpleasant, he had quietly slipped aboard ship and was on his way to America.

Marshal Masséna, defeated in Portugal

Brunswick Troops in the Peninsula

THE INFANTRY

On 8 October 1810 the Brunswick-Oels Jägers, as the infantry regiment was then known, landed in Lisbon. They were apparently twelve companies and a regimental headquarters (H.Q.) strong, and initially went to Pakenham's Brigade in Cole's 4th Division. Shortly after this they were transferred to General Craufurd's Light Division and as part of this formation they took part in the pursuit of Marshal Masséna from the Lines of Torres Vedras on 17 November 1810, and in the skirmish at Santarém (19 November). Other actions in which they participated in the Light Division were Redinka (12 March 1811), Casal Novo (14 March) and Foz d'Arouce (16 March).

After this they were transferred from the Light Division to the newly formed 7th Division which they joined before April 1811. They were in von Alten's Brigade with a strength of the regimental H.Q. and nine companies, the other companies being detached as follows: 4th Division (General Lowry Cole), one company in Ellis's Brigade; 5th Division (General Leith), one company in Greville's Brigade, and one company in Pringle's Brigade. The officers commanding these forma-

tions changed frequently during the war and their names can be found in Oman's excellent *History of the Peninsular War*.

At the battle of Fuentes de Oñoro on 3, 4 and 5 May 1811 the main body of the Brunswickers with the 7th Division were very exposed, positioned as they were on a ford over the Don Casas river at a village called Pozo Velho on the right flank of the British. The 7th Division was an untried polyglot force (the other units in the brigade with the Brunswickers were the 85th Line (British), the 2nd (Portuguese) Caçadores and the Chasseurs Britanniques (a French émigré unit). The 7th Division had not intended to get seriously involved in the battle, but General Marchand's division of Masséna's Army fell upon it and pushed it back on to the main British position. The losses which the Brunswickers suffered are shown in the table on page 16.

After the battle the 7th Division marched into Estremadura and took part in the abortive siege of Badajoz; the Brunswickers suffering casualties in two unsuccessful assaults on the outwork of San Cristobal on the nights of 6 and 9 June. The siege was then lifted due to the approach of a

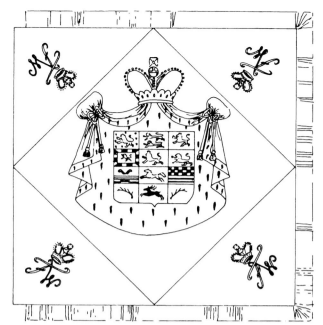

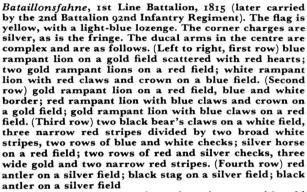

Bataillonsfahne, 1st Line Battalion, 1815 (later carried by the 2nd Battalion 92nd Infantry Regiment). The flag is yellow, with a light-blue lozenge. The corner charges are silver, as is the fringe. The ducal arms in the centre are complex and are as follows. (Left to right, first row) blue rampant lion on a gold field scattered with red hearts; two gold rampant lions on a red field; white rampant lion with red claws and crown on a blue field. (Second row) gold rampant lion on a red field, blue and white border; red rampant lion with blue claws and crown on a gold field; gold rampant lion with blue claws on a red field. (Third row) two black bear's claws on a white field, three narrow red stripes divided by two broad white stripes, two rows of blue and white checks; silver horse on a red field; two rows of red and silver checks, three wide gold and two narrow red stripes. (Fourth row) red antler on a silver field; black stag on a silver field; black antler on a silver field

The arms rest on a scarlet and ermine coat with gold cords; the crown is gold with crimson cushions, ermine band and pearl trim on the arches

At upper right is the *Bataillonsfahne* (reverse), 1st Line Battalion. The flag is yellow with a light-blue lozenge and silver charges.

The gilt tip of the flagstaff is identical to the type used with the *Herzogs Fahne*. A banderole or cravat in silver was worked with round yellow cords

relief force under Soult. The 7th Division had no more combats of note in this year.

In 1812 they were present at the final siege of Badajoz as were the 4th and 5th Divisions whose casualties in the storming attempts are shown in the table on page 16.

The Brunswickers were at the battle of Salamanca on 22 July 1812, but were not heavily engaged and had no casualties. At the battle of Vittoria on 21 June 1813 they suffered some losses and more at the battles of Maya and Roncesvalles on 25 July.

The detached company with the 4th Division was again engaged in the first battle of Sorauren on 28 July and the main body of the regiment lost some men in the second battle of Sorauren on 30 July.

At the skirmish of Echalar on 2 August the main body was again in action, as were the two detached companies in the 5th Division at the siege of St Sebastian on 31 August.

By the time of the crossing of the Bidassoa (7 October) a company of the Brunswick-Oels Jägers was with the 1st Division and both these and their comrades in the 4th Division were engaged that day.

The main body of the Jägers (still in the 7th Division) was engaged in the battles of the Nivella (10 November) and the Nive (9 December). The company in the 5th Division also had losses in this latter battle and on the next day. Their last battle in the Peninsular campaign was that of Orthez on 27 February 1814 where the Brunswickers in the 7th Division were quite heavily involved. The strength of the main body of the Brunswick-Oels Jägers in the 7th Division at the battle of the Nivella was 42 officers and 457 men.

THE HUSSARS

The cavalry of the Black Horde were reorganized into a regiment of hussars which was also sent to Spain, but to the eastern side of the Peninsula where they operated in a force made up largely of foreign levies which was used in amphibious operations along the Spanish coast. This force was commanded by Sir John Murray and included English, Portuguese, Spanish and Italian troops.

LOSSES OF THE BRUNSWICK-OELS JÄGERS IN THE PENINSULA

Battle and Date	Parent formation	Killed		Wounded		Missing		Total
		Officers	Men	Officers	Men	Officers	Men	
Fuentes d'Oñoro 5 May 1811	7th Division	—	1	1	6	—	10	18
Siege of Badajoz 9 June 1811	7th Division	—	1	1	5	—	—	7
Siege of Badajoz 6 April 1812	4th Division 5th Division	—	7	2	26	—	—	35
Battle of Vittoria 21 June 1813	4th Division 5th Division 7th Division	1	—	—	5	—	—	6
Battle of Maya 25 July 1813	7th Division	—	8	3	15	—	15	41
Roncesvalles 25 July 1813	4th Division	—	2	—	2	—	—	4
1st Sorauren 28 July 1813	4th Division	—	1	—	3	—	1	5
2nd Sorauren 30 July 1813	7th Division	—	2	—	1	—	14	17
Skirmish at Echalar 2 Aug. 1813	7th Division	—	1	4	7	—	2	14
Siege of St Sebastian 31 Aug. 1813	5th Division	—	2	1	6	1	5	15
Crossing of the Bidassoa 7 Oct. 1813	1st Division 4th Division	—	7	7	18	—	—	32
Battle of the Nive 9 Dec. 1813	5th Division	—	2	—	1	—	1	4
10 Dec. 1813	5th Division	—	—	1	2	—	—	3
11 Dec. 1813	5th Division	—	1	1	1	—	—	3
Battle of Orthez 27 Feb. 1814	7th Division	2	5	5	32	—	4	48
Totals		3	40	26	130	1	52	252

16

The Brunswick Hussars, two squadrons strong, landed at Alicante, direct from England, in July 1813 and then took part in the raid on Tarragona. This raid, initially very successful, was badly managed by a timid commander and developed into a farce, with a disgracefully, and, unnecessarily, hurried evacuation of the force back on to its ships in which much valuable equipment, including many cannon, was abandoned. Sir John Murray was later court-martialled.

On 25 August 1813 the Brunswick Hussars, with 18 officers and 258 troopers, were part of Lord F. Bentinck's Brigade in this British force on the east coast of Spain. At the combat of Villa Franca on 13 September 1813, they were engaged and lost one officer and eight men, with two officers and twenty-four men wounded and eighteen men missing. In 1814 they took part in the invasion of Sicily.

The 1815 Campaign

The Brunswick-Oels Jägers returned home and left English service on 25 December 1814, but their hussar colleagues remained in English service until mid-1815.

When the Russian and Prussian armies had flooded across north Germany in 1813, the Duke of Brunswick-Oels had been confirmed in his family possessions and at once set about raising new forces which could be used to speed Napoleon's downfall. The first unit raised was a company of Gelernte Jäger which was completed on 1 January 1814. By 16 March 1814 a second company had been formed. Before the year was out Brunswick's forces were:

The Avantgarde of 1815 was divided into two companies of Gelernte Jäger and two light companies. This private is a Gelernte Jäger. His black hat has green brim binding, band, loop, button and plume, and a white metal Saxon horse badge. The grey coat has dark-green facings on collar, shoulder-straps and cuffs, and double stripes on the grey trousers; the gaiters are black. White metal buttons bear the horse motif. The black satchel and bandolier have white metal buckles. The brown powder-horn is slung on a green cord, and has brass furniture, and the rifle sling is black. He carries a *Hirschfanger* bayonet, as in 1809. Brown calfskin packs and round tin canteens were carried. N.C.O.s bore silver rank chevrons on the upper left arm in the British sequence.

Officers' uniforms differed in that the hat had silver edging and a band and plume of drooping dark-green cock's feathers. There were no shoulder-straps and the collar and cuffs had silver lace edging. Officers of the rank of major and up wore a black bandolier and pouch with silver picker equipment and a hunting horn badge. All officers carried a hussar sabre with silver and yellow *Porte-épée*, and wore a silver and yellow waist-sash

LEICHTE-INFANTERIE-BRIGADE

1. *The Avantgarde:* The original infantry of the Black Horde now returned from English service and the two, new Gelernte Jäger companies. There was a total of four companies in the Avantgarde

2. *The Leib-Bataillon:* A new Leib-Bataillon raised from a cadre of the Black Horde and initially known as the 'Leichte-Bataillon von Pröstler' (the name of its commander); on 14 April 1815 this unit became known as the 'Leib-Bataillon'

3. *1st, 2nd and 3rd Leichte-Bataillone:* Newly raised troops

LINIEN-INFANTERIE-BRIGADE

4. *1st, 2nd and 3rd Linien-Infanterie-Bataillone:* Newly raised troops

RESERVE-INFANTERIE-BRIGADE

5. *1st, 2nd, 3rd, 4th and 5th Reserve-Infanterie-Bataillone,* and a type of Landwehr

HUSAREN-REGIMENT

6. This included a squadron of Uhlanen and all men were newly raised troops

ARTILLERIE

7. One foot battery – 8 guns
One horse artillery battery – 8 guns } Newly raised troops
The military train

Apart from the hussars quoted above, the old hussars of the original Black Horde were still in English service. The foot artillery battery had 188 men and the horse artillery battery 227. With the exception of the Reserve-Infanterie-Brigade, these forces were present at Quatre Bras and at Waterloo.

Napoleon left his exile island of Elba on 26 February 1815 and on 1 March he landed between Fréjus and Antibes on the French coast with a force of about a thousand men. The European monarchs were still busy in Vienna, hammering out the post-war map of the Continent, but Bonaparte's reappearance galvanized them into action.

Hat of a private of the Gelernte Jäger companies of the Avantgarde, 1815 (to be seen in the Brunswick Landes-museum). All details are in dark-green, and the horse badge is silver. Knötel illustrates a Gelernte Jäger with the right side of the hat brim turned up (*Uniformenkunde*, Vol. IV, Plate 52). The original hat shown here has the hat brim turned up on the left-hand side and the horse badge facing forward. The Beyer-Pegau pictures show the left side turned up, although many other representations have been based on the Knötel plate

The French Army flocked to rejoin their eagles, Louis XVIII fled to Belgium, and a war-weary Europe took to the business of war again. The armies of Britain, the Netherlands, Prussia, Russia, Austria and their minor allies, were mobilized and divided into six main groups to combat their French adversaries. The northernmost group, and the one with which we shall be most concerned, was a British-Hanoverian-Netherlands-Nassau and Brunswick force of 95,000 men under the Duke of Wellington in Belgium.

To the south-east of this army were 124,000 Prussians under Blücher; 200,000 Russians were advancing on the Saar; Prince Schwarzenberg (the Allied supreme commander) was at the head of 210,000 Austrians advancing via Basle into southern France; and two smaller armies, composed of Austrians and Sardinians, were crossing the Alps from Italy to invade the southernmost parts of France. From their various mobilization points, these armies had different distances to cover in order to close with the enemy, and not all of them were in the same state of readiness for active service. It thus transpired that the armies of Wellington and Blücher were in position in Belgium on the French borders and were ready for action by early June 1815, far in advance of their allies. Schwarzenberg had decided that all his armies should enter France almost simultaneously and thus it was that Wellington and Blücher were instructed to remain inactive until 1 July before advancing.

Napoleon's intelligence service informed him of the dispositions of his enemies and he quickly deduced that his northernmost foes, Wellington and Blücher, were by far the most serious threat to his plans. He thus resolved to attack them first, gain a quick victory (and Brussels, a capital city), and negotiate with his remaining opponents from a strong position.

A potential weakness of the Wellington-Blücher position was that the two army groups had divergent lines of communication. Wellington's lay north-west to the ports of Ostend and Antwerp, and Blücher's lay due east to Prussia. Napoleon recognized this weakness and hoped to exploit it by striking at the junction of the two armies, defeating first one and then the other, causing them to withdraw along their lines of communica-

Private, light companies of the Avantgarde, 1815. The hat is identical to that of the Gelernte Jäger, apart from the white metal hunting horn badge. The private wears a black dolman-style coat with dark-green collar, shoulder-straps and Polish cuffs; the lace, tassels and buttons are black. The trousers are black with a green stripe; the gaiters and leather equipment are black. A steel canteen is strapped to the top of a black canvas pack. N.C.O.s wore the same distinctions as the Gelernte Jäger companies. Officers' hats had drooping plumes of dark-green cock's feathers, and silver – instead of green – decorations. They wore no shoulder-straps, and had silver edging on the cuffs. Weapons and equipment, sash and *Porte-épée* were the same as for officers of the Gelernte Jäger units. Green gloves were worn

their British-Netherlands allies. At the same time, he dispatched Marshal Ney north along the Charleroi–Brussels road to seize and hold the crossroads at Quatre Bras – a vital junction for the co-operation of the two Allied armies opposing him.

At Quatre Bras on 16 June Ney was opposed by a force under the Prince of Orange, son of the King of the Netherlands, and it was here that the Black Brunswickers came under fire again.

Quatre Bras 16 June 1815

The Prince of Orange, a young, rash and inexperienced officer, commanded the I Corps of Wellington's Army and it was troops of this corps which were in possession of the vital crossroads on 15 June when Ney's advanced guard cavalry arrived to take it. After a short fight, Ney called off the attack until the next day. The Netherlands

tion, lose touch with one another and thus endanger their own positions.

On 15 June 1815, the anniversary of the Napoleonic victories of Marengo in 1800 and Friedland in 1807, the French Army crossed the Belgian border near Charleroi and attacked the western flank of the Prussian Army. Wellington and Blücher were taken by surprise, but Blücher (nicknamed 'Marshal Forwards' by his men due to his aggressive and impetuous nature) reacted in character. From his headquarters in Namur he ordered three of his four corps to concentrate at Sombreffe to give battle to the French.

There followed the battle of Ligny on 16 June in which the Prussians were defeated and fell back initially along their lines of communication to the east which was just what Napoleon wanted. In order to ensure that their eastern progress would be maintained, Napoleon sent Marshal Grouchy to follow them up and keep them away from

Marshal Ney, who unsuccessfully led the French at Quatre Bras

forces at Quatre Bras on the 15 June were Colonel Gödecke's 2nd Brigade of de Perponcher's 2nd Dutch-Belgian Division:

2nd Nassau Infantry Regiment	3 battalions or 2,709 men
Regiment of Orange Nassau	2 battalions or 1,591 men
A battery of Dutch Horse Artillery	8 guns

Colonel Gödecke surrendered command of this brigade to Prince Bernhard of Saxe-Weimar on the evening of 15 June.

Ney's forces at Quatre Bras were General Count Reille's Second Corps:

5th Division (Lieutenant-General Baron Bachelu)
2nd Light Infantry Regiment
61st Line Infantry Regiment
72nd Line Infantry Regiment   } 11 battalions
108th Line Infantry Regiment

6th Division (Prince Jerome Napoleon)
1st Light Infantry Regiment
1st Line Infantry Regiment
2nd Line Infantry Regiment   } 11 battalions
3rd Line Infantry Regiment

7th Division (Lieutenant-General Count Girard)
11th Light Infantry Regiment
12th Light Infantry Regiment   } 8 battalions
82nd Line Infantry Regiment

9th Division (Lieutenant-General Count Foy)
4th Light Infantry Regiment
92nd Line Infantry Regiment
93rd Line Infantry Regiment   } 10 battalions
100th Line Infantry Regiment

2nd Cavalry Division (Lieutenant-General Baron Piré)
1st and 6th Chasseurs à Cheval   8 squadrons
5th and 6th Lancers   7 squadrons

Artillery
5 batteries of foot artillery
1 battery of horse artillery   } 46 guns
Engineers

Total	Infantry	19,750[4]
	Cavalry	1,729
	Artillery	1,385
	Engineers	409

The Brunswickers formed their own brigade (commanded by the Black Duke himself) for the Waterloo campaign and were part of Wellington's Reserve.

When news of the French thrust at Quatre Bras reached Wellington, he sent part of the Reserve, including the Brunswickers, to bolster up the weak Netherlands forces there.

The Brunswickers involved were:

The Avantgarde
Two companies of Gelernte Jäger
Two companies of light infantry   } 690 men

The Light Infantry Brigade
The Leib-Bataillon
1st Light Infantry Battalion
2nd Light Infantry Battalion   } 2,965 men
3rd Light Infantry Battalion

The Line Infantry Brigade
1st Line Infantry Battalion
2nd Line Infantry Battalion   } 2,075 men
3rd Line Infantry Battalion

The Cavalry
The Hussar Regiment   } 727 men
Uhlan Squadron   } 246 men

The Artillery
One horse artillery battery of 8 guns   188 men
One foot artillery battery of 8 guns   227 men

The Feldgendarmerie
One commando of Polizei-Husaren   17 men

The artillery and the 1st and 3rd Light Battalions did not reach the battlefield until 6 p.m. that evening.

The Brunswickers arrived on the field of Quatre Bras along the Brussels road at 2.50 p.m. on 16 June and by then, the Netherlands forces there had been reinforced by the following troops:

1st Brigade: 2nd Dutch-Belgian Division of the I Corps (Major-General Count de Bylandt)

7th Line Regiment[5]	701 men
27th Jäger Battalion	809 men
5th Militia Battalion	482 men
7th Militia Battalion	675 men
8th Militia Battalion	566 men
One foot artillery battery	8 guns

Fifty hussars of the 2nd Silesian Hussar Regiment (Prussian Army) had appeared on the field briefly earlier in the day and had rendered valuable service by pushing back the French outposts, but had later returned eastwards to their parent unit and the Prince of Orange had no cavalry under his command.

Les Quatres Bras looking towards Waterloo (National Army Museum)

Recognizing the importance of Quatre Bras, Wellington had sent the 5th Infantry Division from his reserve to bolster up the Prince of Orange's heavily pressed, but gallant, force. Apart from the Brunswickers, the 5th Division, commanded by Lieutenant-General Sir Thomas Picton, included the following troops:

8th British Brigade (Major-General Sir James Kempt)

1st Battalion, 28th Regiment	557 men
1st Battalion, 32nd Regiment	662 men
1st Battalion, 79th Regiment	703 men
1st Battalion 95th Regiment	549 men

9th British Brigade (Major-General Sir Denis Pack)

3rd Battalion 1st Regiment	604 men
1st Battalion 42nd Regiment	526 men
2nd Battalion 44th Regiment	455 men
1st Battalion 92nd Regiment	588 men

4th Hanoverian Brigade (Colonel Best)

Landwehr Battalion Verden	621 men
Landwehr Battalion Lüneburg	624 men
Landwehr Battalion Osterode	677 men
Landwehr Battalion Münden	660 men
Total Infantry	7,226 men

Artillery
British Foot Battery (Major Rogers)
Hanoverian Foot Battery (Hauptmann von Rettberg)

At this time a violent struggle was developing around the farm of St Pierre where the 5th Dutch Militia Battalion was holding out against heavy odds. Finally these young militiamen broke under the continued assault and the French occupied the vital farm.

The 3rd Dutch Light Cavalry Brigade, under General van Merlen, arrived and attempted to restore the situation; but the two regiments (5th Dutch Light Dragoons with 441 sabres, and the 6th Dutch Hussars with 641 sabres) were overthrown by Piré's cavalry and rushed off the battlefield.

As soon as the Brunswickers arrived, they were thrown forward against the farm of St Pierre in an attempt to win back the ground lost by the Dutch. The two Gelernte Jäger companies of the Avantgarde went into the wood at Boussu, while the 2nd Light Battalion was sent over to the left flank of the Allied position near the Materne pond. The main body of the Black Duke's force remained on the Brussels–Charleroi road.

The French began to push forward through the Boussu Woods and Wellington asked the Black Duke to advance towards Germinecourt and extend his right to link up with the Dutch skirmishers. The Leib-Bataillon (under Major

Sergeant-major of the 1st Line Infantry Battalion, 1815. This splendid warrior has a red collar and shoulder-straps, a blue-over-yellow plume, and a sash in the same colours. The shako plate and rank chevrons are silver, and a stick of office is thrust through the frog of the sabre. There is a narrow red stripe on the trousers

Lieutenant of the 1st Line Battalion in undress uniform, 1815. He wears a black cap with red band, black dolman with a red collar and black lace decorations; a red waist-coat with silver lace and buttons, and black trousers with a wide red stripe. The sabre-strap is silver and gold. In the 1809 campaign fatigue caps were worn by all ranks. They were like the cap illustrated here in general shape, but were without peaks and had floppy, unstiffened crowns. The headbands were light-blue throughout the corps and were about 2 in. wide. Officers had silver decorations on the blue bands, and the Black Duke himself wore a band of silver laurel leaves above the blue band

Pröstler), the 1st Line Battalion (Major Metzner) and the two light infantry companies of the Avantgarde, advanced, the latter linking up in a skirmishing line with their colleagues, the Gelernte Jäger, in Boussu Wood. Directly behind the infantry were the Brunswick Hussars (Major Cramm) and the Brunswick Uhlan Squadron (Major Pott). The 2nd and 3rd Line Battalions remained, as a reserve, in front of Quatre Bras itself.

The French were now preparing a general assault on Quatre Bras and the 5th British Division was being subjected to a very telling cannonade. To forestall this assault, the Duke of Wellington decided to attack the enemy and pre-empt the French blow. Despite heavy French fire this assault of Kempt and Pack's brigades was success-ful and the French line was thrown back across the valley by the Materne pond.

Meanwhile, the French were raking the exposed Brunswickers with artillery and skirmisher fire and their losses were mounting, particularly among the hussars. Although the members of the old Black Horde had been taken into the service of the newly re-formed forces of the Black Duke, they had been relatively few in number and had been split up among all the units in order to supply cadres of experienced men to which the new recruits could be attached. Thus the great majority of each battalion was made up of new, raw recruits and this was even more true of the hussars and Uhlans. The Black Duke himself was very much aware of the brittle nature of the morale of his men and he sought to maintain their spirits, despite their considerable casualties, by calmly walking up and down in front of them, smoking his pipe in the fury of the battle. He also requested some artillery from the Duke of Wellington so that he might at least reply to that of the enemy. Four guns arrived and were set up to the right of the Brunswickers, but two of these were quickly put out of action by well-aimed enemy fire. A mass of Jerome's infantry began to advance northwards along the Brussels road, extending to the Boussu Wood, and pushing the Dutch-Belgian and Brunswick skirmishers before them. In an effort to impede this advance, the Black Duke charged the French at the head of his Uhlan Squadron, but this faint hope was dashed to failure by the musketry of the enemy infantry and the Uhlans fell back to Quatre Bras with heavy losses. The advance of Jerome's troops continued and the Brunswick infantry were also pushed back to the vital crossroads. The Leib-Bataillon was hotly pursued by the enemy, and a telling volley of artillery fire finally broke the young troops' composure and they fled back to Quatre Bras in spite of Major Pröstler's efforts to rally them.

It was at this point that the Black Duke, also trying to re-form his men, was struck by a musket ball which penetrated his hand, body and liver. The time was 6 p.m. He died within minutes, his only words being to his aide, Major von Wachholtz, 'Mein lieber Wachholtz, wo ist denn Olfermann?' ('My dear Wachholtz, where is Olfermann?') [6]

The Brunswick Hussars were then ordered forward to counter Piré's light cavalry which was also advancing on Quatre Bras, but they were outnumbered and subjected to heavy musket fire as they advanced unsupported, and were also overthrown and pursued. The Brunswickers rallied at the Quatre Bras crossroads and successfully held up further advances on this sector while on the Allied left flank the 95th British Regiment and the 2nd Brunswick Light Battalion effectively stopped French outflanking attempts there.

The Allied cavalry, being greatly inferior in numbers and quality to that of the French, the British and their allies, was continuously subjected to heavy cavalry attacks. These, however, were usually beaten off in the traditional British manner, the 42nd Regiment (Black Watch) even capturing part of a French lancer regiment which

Herzogs Fahne, **3rd Line Battalion, 1815. Both sides were the same – light-blue, with narrow silver lace edging and silver devices. The crown tip of the flagstaff is gilt, and the cravat is gold with light-blue silk cord decoration**

Captain of the 1st Line Battalion in the service dress he would have worn at Waterloo. The feather plume is blue-over-yellow, the shako plate is silver, the collar and trouser stripe are red; all lace and decorations on the dolman are black. The waist-sash and sabre-strap are silver and gold, and the sabre is in a steel sheath

1st British Division was ordered into the Boussu Wood which they speedily cleared of the French light troops who had threatened the British right for so long. The Brunswick Leib-Bataillon joined this advance of the British Guards of Maitland's Brigade and formed on the left of their line as they prepared to advance against the French infantry between the Boussu Wood and the Charleroi road. A sudden rush of French cavalry was noticed to their flank, but both British and Brunswickers saved themselves by their cool action: the British Guards simply moved into the ditch along the edge of Boussu Wood while the Brunswickers quickly formed square and poured a deadly flanking volley into the cavalry. This was followed by more fire from the British Guards and the shattered cavalry fled the field.

Wellington now outnumbered Ney by about 28,000 to 18,000 and he ordered a general advance which pushed the French off the field. Ney withdrew to the heights of Frasne, but Wellington did not pursue him because he had not heard of Blücher's progress at Ligny. It had been a hard battle and the Brunswickers had borne much of the brunt of the fighting throughout the whole long day.

Siborne gives total losses (dead, wounded and missing) on the Allied side as:

British	2,275
Hanoverians	369
Brunswickers	819
	3,463

penetrated their square as it was in act of formation! The Hanoverian Landwehr Battalion Verden was not so lucky and was caught in line by another French lancer attack, with the result that it was almost completely destroyed.

Meanwhile, Ney was still desperately trying to break the Allied line, but gradual reinforcements which joined Wellington from his rear were slowly tipping the balance.

The Brunswick artillery and the 1st and 3rd Light Infantry Battalions arrived on the field about one hour later; the guns were set up to the left of Quatre Bras and the infantry reinforced their countrymen (the 1st and 3rd Line Battalions) in the houses of Quatre Bras. The newly arrived

The official Brunswick dispatch concerning the battle, however, gives the casualty figures for Quatre Bras as follows:

	Killed	Wounded	Total
Officers	3	23	26
Men	185	373	558
	188	396	584

No mention is made of missing personnel. Singled out for special commendation in this official report were the Leib-Bataillon, the 2nd Light Battalion and the 2nd Line Battalion.

1 Trooper, Hussar Regiment, 1809
2 Soldier, Infantry Regiment, 1809
3 Officer, Infantry Regiment, 1809

A

1 Trumpeter, Hussar Regiment, 1809
2 Sharpshooter, 1809
3 Officer, Hussar Regiment, 1809

B

1 Trooper, Uhlan Squadron, 1809
2 Officer, Sharpshooters, 1809
3 Soldier, Infantry Regiment in English
  service, 1809–15

C

1 Sergeant, Leib-Bataillon, 1815
2 Trooper, Hussar Regiment in English service, 1809–15
3 Captain, Hussar Regiment in English service, 1809–15

D

1 Officer, Infantry Regiment in English
   service, 1809–15
2 Officer, Leib-Bataillon, 1815
3 Sharpshooter, Infantry Regiment in English
   service, 1809–15

E

1 Sergeant-Major, 2nd Light Battalion, 1815
2 Private, 3rd Light Battalion, 1815
3 Private, 2nd Line Battalion, 1815

F

1 Senior Musician, 1st Line Battalion, 1815
2 Junior Officer, 2nd Line Battalion, 1815
3 Drummer, 1st Line Battalion, 1815

G

1 Drum Major, 2nd Line Battalion, 1815
2 Officer, Horse Artillery Battery, 1815
3 Driver, Train of Foot Artillery, 1815

Waterloo 18 June 1815

Hearing finally of Blücher's defeat at Ligny and his intended withdrawal northwards in a final attempt to stop Napoleon at Waterloo, Wellington pulled his forces back from Quatre Bras on 17 June and deployed them along the ridge across the Charleroi–Brussels road at Mont St Jean; a position which he had had in mind for just such an eventuality.

The Brunswick Corps (now commanded by Oberst Olfermann after the death of the Black Duke) was in the Allied Reserve and, at the start of the day, they were positioned about half a mile due north of the farm of Hougoumont, in the second line of Allied troops. The left of the corps rested on the Nivelles road; the Avantgarde-Bataillon was detached to the right of the village of Merbe Braine. All units of the Brunswick Corps were present on the field that morning. The strength of the corps, according to Siborne, was:

Infantry	4,586
Cavalry	866
Artillery	510 with 16 guns
	5,962

The Brunswickers were split into three parts for the duration of Waterloo. The cavalry operated with other Allied cavalry units. The Avantgarde, the Leib-Bataillon and the 1st Light Battalion were posted at the north-west corner of Hougoumont, in support of the garrison there, and the 2nd and 3rd Light Battalions and the three line battalions, together with the artillery, were initially in reserve in the second line of the Allied position. The garrison of Hougoumont consisted of Byng's Guards Brigade. Their immediate opponents on the western half of the battlefield were once again to be the forces under Ney with

Hougoumont looking towards Waterloo (National Army Museum)

La Haye Sainte looking towards Waterloo (National Army Museum)

whom they had fought so desperately at Quatre Bras two days before. The battle commenced at about 11.30 a.m. when Reille's Corps began an attack on Hougoumont.

For about three hours this battle, one of the bloodiest and yet most magnificent spectacles of modern history, raged across the valley between the opposing lines before the Brunswickers were seriously involved.

It was the occasion of the second, massive French cavalry attack (Napoleon's first ponderous assault on the Allied left at Papelotte had been bloodily repulsed). The immortal charge of the Union Brigade had scattered the French assault columns and had, in turn, been badly mauled by Napoleon's lancers when the British cavalry had over-extended themselves and had dared to venture among the gunners of the cannon on the main French position. Repeated attacks on La Haye Sainte and Hougoumont had been thrown back, but now Ney mounted an awe-inspiring show of force in the form of a mass of cavalry directed against the Allied right.

The cavalry consisted of Milhaud's twenty-four squadrons of cuirassiers, Lefèbvre Desnouette's Light Cavalry Division of the Guard (seven squadrons of Red Lancers and twelve squadrons of Chasseurs à Cheval de la Garde). They ascended the hill on which the main Allied line was based, flooded over the cannon to the front of it and pushed on to attack the Allied infantry, drawn up in squares on the reverse slope of the hill and ready to meet this cavalry attack.

There was general apprehension among the Allied commanders, and troops, as to how these generally raw young soldiers would conduct themselves under such a heavy attack after having suffered quite heavily at Quatre Bras only two days before. But no one need have worried: the Brunswickers behaved as well as any veteran British unit. The attack was driven off and the Brunswick Hussars and Lancers took part in the Allied counter-attack which hastened the Frenchmen on their way out of the Allied line.

Gathering once more, the French cavalry attacked again and a cavalry battle developed on the Allied position between part of the French assaulting force and Somerset's Cavalry Brigade supported by the 23rd British Light Dragoons, Trip's Dutch-Belgian Carabinier Brigade, the Brunswick Hussars and Uhlans, the 1st Light Dragoons of the King's German Legion and the 7th British Hussars.

The French cavalry outnumbered the Allies by about two to one, but this was balanced somewhat by the fire of the Allied infantry squares on the flank and rear of the French masses. After a bloody fight the French fell back. Among the other regiments engaged, the Brunswickers were commended for their bravery in this action.

The French cavalry carried out the same fruitless exercise of repeatedly throwing themselves at the Allied squares. The original mass of French cavalry was reinforced by Kellerman's Heavy Cavalry Corps (the divisions of L'Heritier and Roussel d'Urbal totalling seven squadrons of dragoons, eleven of cuirassiers and six of carabiniers), expressly at Napoleon's command. Ney also pulled in more forces, namely Guyot's Heavy Cavalry Division of the Guard (six squadrons of horse grenadiers and seven of dragoons). These thirty-seven squadrons joined the remains of the original forty-three and threw themselves yet again at the British right wing, which was

The Duke of Wellington (National Army Museum)

dangerously weak in cavalry. The squares held; the French cavalry frittered away their strength in profitless charges, were held, assailed from all sides, and finally thrown back by the Allied cavalry, which waited in rear of the squares until the order and momentum of the French attack was destroyed and then swept them off the Allied position.

The farm of La Haye Sainte, held heroically for hours against tremendous odds by Major Baring's men of the King's German Legion, had to be surrendered to the enemy as Baring had run out of ammunition. This unfortunate lapse in the supply system is still unclear, even more so since Baring had twice asked urgently for ammunition and had received neither ammunition nor any explanation for its absence.

Shortly before this, Lieutenant-Colonel Dickson's British Horse Battery, commanded by Major Mercer, was brought into position in front of the Brunswick infantry to reinforce that part of the line as a precaution against a threatening new attack. These guns were soon at work wreaking

Sash of a junior officer, 1st Light Battalion, 1815. It is silver with seven longitudinal stripes of gold, each about ½ in. wide, with the intervening silver stripes each about ¾ in. wide. Whip and tassels are silver

carnage on an attempted assault by the horse grenadiers and cuirassiers. It is in the subsequent Allied counter-attack, that the charges of cowardice are laid against Trip's Dutch-Belgian Carabiniers and the Hanoverian Cumberland Hussars. The former, after having been personally exhorted to attack by Lord Uxbridge, fled at the approach of the enemy, while the latter calmly left the field without being engaged, their commanding officer (Colonel Hake) declaring that he had no confidence in his men; they were volunteers, their horses were their own property, and so on!

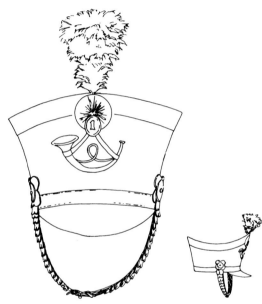

Officer's shako, 1st Light Battalion, 1815. The body is of black felt; the peak, top and chin-scales are black leather. The top band is black velvet, the cockade black silk and the badge is silver; the feather plume is yellow-over-blue

The fall of La Haye Sainte caused the French to redouble their efforts on the centre of the Allied line and on Hougoumont. The bloody business went on much as before, with all the fury and bravery of the French assaults being shattered on the stolid Allied defence.

Some Prussians of Zieten's advanced guard had appeared on the British left, but it was clear that Wellington's men would have to face the gathering French assault on their own. In view of his reduced strength, Wellington made some redispositions of his troops, including the movement of the Brunswick infantry from behind the brigades of Maitland and Adam, to their left to the interval between Halkett's British Brigade and Kruse's Nassau Brigade.

Now was to come the moment of the assault of the Imperial Guard – Napoleon's last throw for victory, a gamble which was to be shattered by the fire and the steadiness of the 1st Regiment of Foot Guards and the 52nd Regiment of the Line. It was for this action that the 1st Guards received their current title of 'Grenadier Guards'. Some believe that the laurels for this victory should rightly have gone to the 52nd Regiment.

As the French columns advanced, the Prince of Orange put himself at the head of Kruse's Nassau Brigade and charged them, but he was wounded and the attack failed. The Brunswick infantry (2nd and 3rd Light and 1st, 2nd and 3rd Line Battalions) was ordered to support the Nassauers, but were also forced back about one hundred yards by the weight of the assault. At this critical moment, when the centre of the British line seemed about to break, Wellington rode up and addressed himself to the Brunswickers. They rallied and held up a further enemy advance in this sector. Ammunition was running low, however, and one of the Brunswick battalions had none left at all. But the crisis soon passed as the enemy pressure there slackened. In Plancenoit, on the Allied left, the Prussians were engaged in considerable numbers, and it was clear that Napoleon's plan of divide and conquer had failed. The Allies had joined up and the French defeat was certain. Wellington realized what a tremendously adverse affect on the French morale the defeat of the legendary and invincible Imperial Guard would have and he commanded a rapid counter-attack to follow up the retreating giants in order to increase the disorder and confusion which was sure to break out in the French ranks. With a great cheer the Allied line swept forward, preceded by Vivian's Hussar Brigade which succeeded in breaking up the French reserve cavalry before them.

The rapidly setting sun threw a symbolic, blood-red glow over the scene of unequalled carnage, and as it slipped slowly below the horizon so Napoleon's star, so long in the heavens over Europe, sank to its long-awaited end.

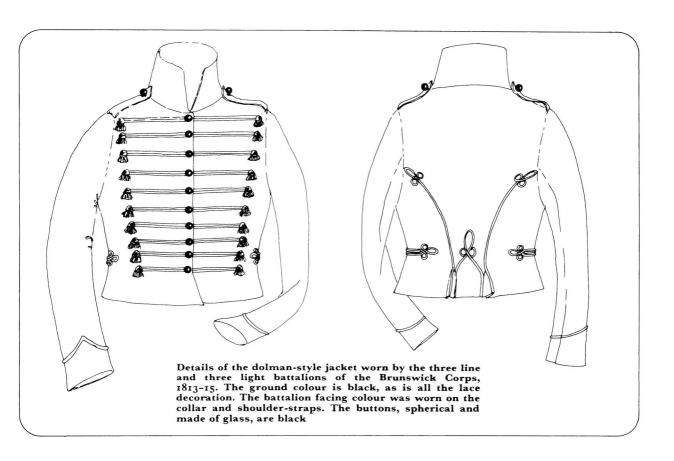

Details of the dolman-style jacket worn by the three line and three light battalions of the Brunswick Corps, 1813-15. The ground colour is black, as is all the lace decoration. The battalion facing colour was worn on the collar and shoulder-straps. The buttons, spherical and made of glass, are black

As is well known, the pursuit proper of the beaten French Army was given over to the Prussian Army, the Anglo-Allied Army having halted on the original French position and to the west of the Brussels–Quatre Bras road in order to clear the way for their allies. After the tremendous exertions of the day the men of Wellington's sorely tried army bivouacked on the battlefield amid scenes of heart-breaking slaughter, death, damage and valour.

Siborne gives the losses of the Brunswickers at Waterloo as:

	Killed	Wounded	Missing
Officers	7	26	—
N.C.O.s and men	147	430	50
Horses	77	—	—

The casualties among the other ranks of the Brunswick forces engaged at Quatre Bras and Waterloo were as follows according to casualty returns in the Brunswick Landesmuseum:

	Dead	Wounded	Missing
Hussar Regiment	16	45	40
Uhlan Squadron	4	12	15
Horse Artillery Battery	2	4	2
Train Company	—	1	—
Avantgarde	20	70	45
Leib-Bataillon	41	145	29
1st Light Infantry Battalion	6	31	34
2nd Light Infantry Battalion	54	110	39
3rd Light Infantry Battalion	53	160	57
1st Line Infantry Battalion	25	98	54
2nd Line Infantry Battalion	25	164	31
3rd Line Infantry Battalion	14	68	31
Foot Artillery Battery	—	6	1
Train Company	—	4	—
	260	918	378

The campaign of Waterloo came to a fairly rapid end; Napoleon's position as emperor crumbled as soon as his military situation ceased to be impregnable; Paris capitulated on 3 July 1815 and effective French resistance ceased. Napoleon went into his final exile on St Helena and Louis XVIII was once more thrust on to the unwilling French nation by force of Allied bayonets.

The Germans in general received high praise for their conduct at Waterloo, particularly the King's German Legion and some of the Hanoverians. The Brunswickers had their fair share

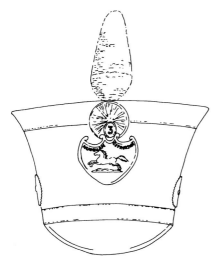

Detail of the shako of a ranker of the 3rd Line Battalion, 1815. The flat-topped shako is of black felt, trimmed top and bottom with black leather and with a black leather cockade. The worsted pompon is light-blue-over-yellow, the chin scales and bosses are of black leather, the badge is silver. There is no metal edge to the black peak

of this glory, justly won and paid for in the blood they shed in those few momentous days in 1815.

The Brunswick troops later formed the 92nd Infantry Regiment and the 17th Hussar Regiment of the Prussian Army from 1866 to 1918.

The death's-head badge was retained as the cap-badge of the Brunswick Hussars as were the battle honours won during the period 1809–15 namely: 'PENINSULAR' and 'WATERLOO'

There were thus three hussar regiments in the German Army of 1914–18 who wore a skull-and-crossbones badge; these were the 1st and 2nd Regiments of Leibhusaren and the Brunswickers.

Lancer (left) and officer of the Uhlanen, 1815. The cut remained as it had been in 1809, but the colours are as follows. Chapka: black skull, black peak with brass edge, yellow band dividing skull from top; light-blue top with yellow piping up the four corners and across the top. Kurtka: black with light-blue collar, shoulder-straps, cuffs, lapels, turnbacks and piping on rear of sleeve and rear seams of jacket; yellow buttons, black *Passgurtel* with light-blue edge. The breeches are black with wide single light-blue side-stripes for troopers, twin stripes for officers. There is a black leather reinforcement. The lance, previously brown, is now black with a light-blue-over-yellow pennant. The officer's chapka has a gold lace band between skull and top, and silver cords. For parades, tall, drooping blue-over-yellow feather plumes were attached. Officers' epaulettes had light-blue straps and gilt crescents, held by silver shoulder-loops and gold buttons. Their bandoliers were gold with silver picker equipment, the buckles silver, the cartouche black with gilt edging and *FW* cipher. Sashes and sabre-knots were silver and yellow. N.C.O.s were distinguished by one or two silver chevrons lining the top of the Polish cuffs

1. The order of battle for the polyglot contingents of the Holy Roman Empire was decided on the basis of the seniority of the proprietors of each unit in the Imperial hierarchy – most senior on the right of the line, and the remainder ranged in descending order of seniority to the left. If any unit's proprietor was promoted or fell from favour, its place in the physical line of battle had to be changed immediately.

2. In all, Mack had 70,000 Austrian soldiers under command. Some 20,000, mostly infantry, capitulated with him at Ulm. Most of the remainder were scattered or captured within a few days thereafter. Napoleon's force for this operation totalled 210,000 men.

3. Like most of their European contemporaries, the Austrians used the Gregorian calendar, while the Russians used the Julian – with a twelve-day difference. Thus Mack expected the Russians to link up with him at Ulm on day X, while the Russians planned on arriving on X plus 12!

4. The 7th Division was not on the field of Quatre Bras and thus the infantry total of the II Corps was actually 16,189 men.

5. The 7th Dutch Line Regiment, with 701 men, was part of the 1st Brigade, but arrived late on the field of Quatre Bras at about 6 p.m.

6. Olfermann was the colonel commanding the Brunswick Brigade.

7. Jurgen Olmes in Plate 76 of his series 'Heere der Vergangenheit' shows an infantry private (Fig. 1) and an officer (Fig. 2) with light-blue cuffs. As justification he quotes Article 5 of the Vienna Convention which laid down that the uniform of the corps was to be 'Schwarz mit lichtblauen Aufschlägen' (black with light-blue facings or cuffs) 'Aufschlag' is a confusing word meaning either 'cuff' or 'facings' and, without further illustration either verbal or pictorial, it is impossible to decipher which is intended.

In the seventeenth century the inter-regimental distinguishing colours were worn, initially, only on the cuffs of the coat, as lapels and collars often did not exist. When these latter items came into use they were often in the colour of the cuff (Aufschlag) thus 'cuff' and 'facings' are almost synonymous.

Olmes also states that other (pictorial) sources show these cuffs to have been black and quotes Kortzfleisch, R. Knötel and H. Knötel. These latter sources are recognized as being extremely reliable and to this list I would also add A. Beyer-Pegau a Saxon artist who between 1898 and 1904 painted a series of over one hundred water-colours of Brunswick's troops from the eighteenth century to 1870. These paintings were based on actual uniform items in the Brunswick Landesmuseum and are approximately 12 in. × 18 in. in size. The detail and artistry are magnificent. Beyer-Pegau shows black cuffs and there is no doubt that his pictures were used as source material by the Knötels. Considering all these facts I would think that black cuffs would be the most likely answer.

8. From examples of actual shakos in the Brunswick Landesmuseum, it is clear that various types were in use in the period 1813–15. Some were of the 1812 Russian *Kiwer* type with the dished or concave top, and others were flat-topped, more like the Prussian model.

SOURCES

Bain, N., *A Detailed Account of the Battles of Quatre Bras, Ligny and Waterloo* (Edinburgh 1819).

Beyer-Pegau, E., Collection of water-colours in the Brunswick Landesmuseum.

Boulger, D. C., *The Belgians at Waterloo* (London 1901).

The Elberfeld Collection.

Fiebig, E., *Unsterbliche Treue* (Berlin 1936).

Herold, J. C., *The Battle of Waterloo* (London 1967).

Knötel, R., Uniform Plates 32 and 33, Vol. I; 52 and 53, Vol. IV; 28, Vol. V; 18, Vol, XVII.

Knötel-Sieg, *Handbuch der Uniformkunde* (Hamburg 1906).

The Lipperheide Collection (Berlin).

Olmes, J., *Armies of the Past* (Plate 76).

Pflugk-Harttung, *Belle-Alliance (Verbundetes Heer)* (Berlin 1915).

Schirmer, F., *Die Zinnfigur* (Neue folge, 8. Jahrgang, Heft 8/15 August 1959).

Siborne, *The Waterloo Campaign 1815* (Birmingham 1894).

Zeitschrift für Heereskunde

Exhibits and documents in the Brunswick Landes-museum.

The Plates

A1 Trooper, Hussar Regiment, 1809

The shako is identical to that of the infantryman, but with brass chin-scales. A black dolman is worn, without shoulder-straps, but with a light-blue collar of infantry dimensions. The light-blue pointed cuffs are sewn only to the outer face of the sleeve, the inner face being black. The chest bears fourteen rows of round black lace, without terminal tassels, and five rows of spherical black glass buttons. The seams on the back and sleeves of the dolman are decorated with the same type of lace. Most pictures of the period show the hussars wearing black overalls with leather inserts, brass buttons and narrow light-blue side piping. The hussar boots have straight-necked, screwed-in steel spurs.

A yellow cord waist-sash is worn, with light-blue barrels, a yellow whip and tassel fringes, and light-blue runners and tassel body. The black leather bandolier has a brass rosette, chains and picker-plate; the black leather cartouche bears a white metal skull and crossbones. The sabre is of Austrian light cavalry pattern, with steel hilt and sheath; the leather fist-strap, slings, and waist-belt are black and the latter has a simple steel snake clasp. Plain black leather sabretaches hang on three straps. Greatcoats, when made up, were mid-calf length, with a high collar, and a cape collar extending to just above the wrist. As with the infantry, N.C.O.s' distinctions are unclear but were probably limited to the sabre-strap.

A2 Soldier, Infantry Regiment, 1809

The shako, though Austrian supplied, is not the normal Austrian infantry pattern. Contemporary paintings show that it is of black felt, larger at the top than at the headband, with black leather top, headband, peak and chin-strap. Above the white metal skull-and-crossbones badge worn on the front centre is a circular black leather cockade

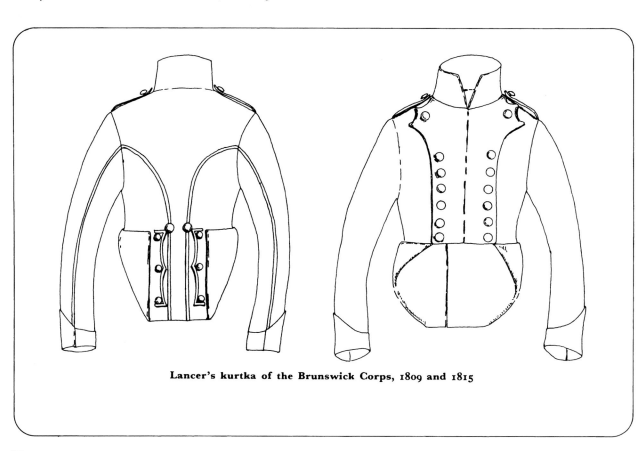

Lancer's kurtka of the Brunswick Corps, 1809 and 1815

Sabre-strap (*Porte-épée*) of a senior Brunswick officer, 1815. The strap is silver with two narrow gold stripes running along it, the body and outer fringe of the tassel are silver; the inner fringe is gold

extending to the top of the shako. Originally there had been a black feather plume, but this is of horsehair on a stiff centre-piece, about one and a quarter times the height of the shako; it is constructed so that from the knot of horsehair at the top a tuft of short hairs stick up, and long strands droop down to the level of the peak.

The coat is the *Polrock* or *Litewka*, the national dress of Lithuania, which was to become so popular among German volunteer units in 1813. Black, single-breasted and reaching to just above the knee, it has a standing collar reaching the lobes of the ears, worn open at the front in the Austrian style; the collar of the 1st and 2nd Battalions is light-blue, that of the 3rd, yellow. Sources differ as to whether the pointed cuffs are black, or follow the collar shade. By modern standards the shoulders of the *Litewka* are narrow, and the sleeves – which come up partially over the point of the shoulder – have a slightly puffed appearance. No shoulder-straps are shown. The breast is covered by six rows of round black lace extending from waist to collar; each row is of equal length, and terminates in black tassels. The coat is closed with six black toggles, in the manner of modern duffel coats. There are no turnbacks on the *Litewka*, no visible pockets and no other ornamentation; there is a single, central rear vent.

The simplicity of the garment is probably due to considerations of practical economy.

Plain black trousers, with a light-blue side-stripe of about $\frac{1}{4}$ in. are worn over shoes and black buttoned gaiters. Black cross-belts support a black Austrian cartridge pouch without badge over the left shoulder; and over the right, the bayonet scabbard. Two black shoulder-straps united by a chest-strap support the brown calfskin Austrian pack, with three steel buckles. A grey drill haversack was usually slung over the right shoulder, and the soldier carries a glass water-bottle in a wicker cover.

There were few obvious differences between men and N.C.O.s. The latter carried sabres as well as bayonets, but sticks of office were not carried. Junior and senior N.C.O.s were probably differentiated by different patterns of sabre fist-strap, although this is not certain. The hair was cut short, and moustaches were worn. It may be speculated that drummers of the corps wore light-blue and black 'swallows' nests' on the shoulder, with the senior or battalion's drummer perhaps wearing 'swallows' nests' in light-blue and silver – but no firm confirmation for this has come to light.

A3 Officer, Infantry Regiment, 1809
Apart from the superior quality of their clothes and equipment, officers' distinctions are few. The only difference from the shako is the addition of silver chin-scales. Flanking each of the six central toggles on the chest are two other toggles, midway out towards the tassels at the ends of the rows of lace. White gloves are worn. A light cavalry sabre is carried with three-bar steel hilts, black grips and black and steel sheaths. The waist-belt and slings are black, with silver lion's-head buckles. The *Port-épée* or sabre-knot is silver.

B1 Trumpeter, Hussar Regiment, 1809
Beyer-Pegau[7] shows a trumpeter of hussars in 1809. The dress differs from the trooper's in that there are 'swallows' nests' in gold and black with a gold fringe along the bottom (perhaps Beyer-Pegau painted the regimental trumpeter), white gloves and a brass trumpet with cords and tassels in yellow and light-blue.

The dark-green coat is closed with two parallel rows each of nine yellow buttons; collar, cuffs, shoulder-straps and turnbacks are red. The collar is the standing, open-fronted type, and the straight 'Swedish' cuffs have one button in the rear top corner. Long grey or white trousers are worn, over shoes and black gaiters. This sharpshooter carries his personal effects in a black leather satchel (*Ranzentasche*), slung on the left hip by a bandolier over the right shoulder, as is the black leather sheath of the white-handled sword-bayonet (*Hirschfänger*). A green cord over the shoulder supports the brown powder-horn with brass fittings. The short rifle has a light-brown sling.

Field officer of the 2nd Line Battalion in undress uniform, 1815. He wears a dark-green headband on the black cap, dark-green collar on the black dolman, dark-green waist-coat with silver lace and buttons, wide dark-green trouser stripe, and elaborate silver Hungarian knots on the sleeves of the dolman above the black cuffs to indicate the rank of major and above

B2 Sharpshooter, 1809

During the occupation of Leipzig in 1809, a Gelernten Jäger oder Scharfschützen Kompanie (Experienced Rifle or Sharpshooter Company) was raised; on 23 June it had a strength of 4 officers and 180 Jägers. The uniform appears to have been a curious mixture of Prussian and Austrian items, the coat being similar to that worn by Prussian füsiliers of the day, while the hats were Austrian Jäger pattern.

The black 'Corsican' hat has a wide green band; the left-hand brim is extended and turned up so that it is higher than the crown. Apparently there was no badge, cockade or other decoration.

Private of the 3rd Line Battalion in field service marching kit, 1815. His uniform has a light-blue-over-yellow pom-pon, silver shako plate, a black dolman-style jacket with white collar and shoulder-straps and white trouser-seam piping. The lace, buttons and leather equipment are all black; the water-canteen is a light-blue wooden item of British issue

B3 Officer, Hussar Regiment, 1809

The shako is the same as that of the infantry officer. Instead of a dolman, hussar officers wear the same pattern of black *Polrock* or *Litewka* as infantry officers but with six rows of round black lace, terminating in black tassels, across the chest; it is closed by six black toggles. The collar is light-blue, the cuffs black. Around the waist officers wear yellow silk hussar-pattern sashes with silver barrels, runners and tassel. The bandolier and pouch are the same pattern as those of troopers, but of better quality, and the black sabretache bears a silver death's-head badge. Silver lions' heads flank the clasp of the black waist-belt, and the steel-hilted sabre is carried in a black and silver sheath on black slings. The sabre-knot is as for infantry officers, and white gloves are worn. The black overalls have a narrow light-blue side piping, silver buttons and black leather inserts. The screwed-in spurs are silver.

Horse harness was black leather, of Hungarian pattern, with white metal fittings. Other ranks had black sheepskin saddle-covers with light-blue wolf's-tooth edging; officers had black cloth shabracks with pointed rear corners and a wide light-blue edging. Saddles were of the old Turkish or 'Bock' type, of birch and leather.

C1 Trooper, Uhlan Squadron, 1809

The formation of this unit was begun in Dresden, and the squadron joined the duke's forces at Zwickau on 23 July 1809. Their uniform is almost an exact copy of that of the Austrian Graf von Meerveldt Uhlanen Regiment, apart from the small death's-head badge on the chapka.

The chapka is yellow at the top, with a black leather skull and peak; there is no cockade or plume, but a small white metal death's-head is worn low on the front, and there are yellow cords. The jacket is a typical lancer kurtka of traditional Polish cut, in dark-green with ponceau red facings on the collar, pointed cuffs, lapels, shoulder-straps, turnbacks and piping on rear of sleeves and back of jacket. The buttons are yellow. The dark-green overalls have yellow buttons, red piping and black leather reinforcement. The black boots have short, straight-necked, screw-in steel spurs. Around the waist there is a wide dark-green and red sash (*Passgurtel*) and under the jacket a

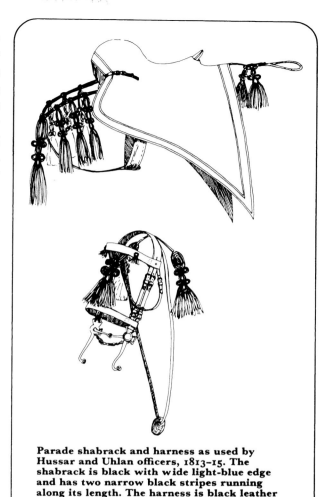

Parade shabrack and harness as used by Hussar and Uhlan officers, 1813–15. The shabrack is black with wide light-blue edge and has two narrow black stripes running along its length. The harness is black leather with brass buckles. (Stirrups and double reins are omitted here for clarity.) The exotic leather furniture, of traditional Polish design, seems to have been largely to help the horse keep flies at bay

black leather waist-belt supporting a sabre of the pattern carried by the hussars. The bandolier and pouch are also of hussar pattern, and armament is augmented by a wooden lance with a steel head and shoe and a red and yellow pennant. Apparently the Uhlanen did not carry carbines.

Officers wore a uniform generally similar but of better quality. They wore gold epaulettes instead of the red shoulder-straps, and at the rear of the waist was the so-called 'waterfall' made up of gold tassels. White gloves were worn.

Shabracks were green with red edging and long, pointed rear corners. All other horse furniture was for the hussars.

Infantrymen of the 2nd and 3rd Line Battalions and 2nd Light Battalion; and (foreground) drummer of 1st Line Battalion and officer of 3rd Light Battalion

C2 Officer, Sharpshooters, 1809
Officers of this unit wear the infantry officers' shako with death's-head badge, but instead of the black horsehair plume they wear a drooping plume of black cock's feathers. The long-skirted green frock-coat, with a woven gold aiguilette on the right shoulder, has buttons and facings as for the Jägers. Long grey trousers are worn over shoes; and the infantry officers' belt and sabre are worn.

Brunswick-Oels Troops in English service, 1810–15
Although certain minor items of uniform and equipment changed from Austrian pattern to English, the main colour scheme of the Black Horde's uniforms was retained. They received the English system of rank chevrons for other ranks, worn in silver on the right upper arm; and also English muskets, bayonets, pouches, canvas packs and water-canteens. Officers adopted the British crimson silk waist-sash, the gold and crimson sword-knot, and the cipher *GR* on their appointments.

C3 Soldier Infantry Regiment in English service, 1809–15
The shako is unchanged from that of the 1809 campaign. The *Polrock* has given way to a short, dolman-like tunic in black, with black cuffs, black lace and toggles on the chest, and a light-blue collar. The black trousers worn over shoes and short black gaiters, have a narrow light-blue side piping. The brown-painted canvas pack is decorated with a white horse and in black the motto, *Nunquam Retrorsum*. A grey greatcoat is carried rolled on top of the pack. Black bandoliers support a plain black cartridge pouch and a black bayonet scabbard. The round wooden canteen, of British issue, is painted light-blue and marked in white, B.L.J., for 'Braunschweig Lauenburg'sche Jäger'. The white canvas haversack (obscured here) and 'Brown Bess' musket are also of British issue.

N.C.O.s were uniformed as the other ranks, apart from silver chevrons on the right arm, crimson waist-sashes with a central stripe in

Officers (left and centre) and trooper, Uhlan Squadron, 1815

light-blue, and they carried sabres as well as bayonets.

Drummers had 'swallows' nests' in light-blue and black. They carried no weapon apart from a sabre. The drum sling and apron were black; the drumsticks were black, held in a square brass plate on the sling. The brass drum had light-blue and yellow hoops.

D1 Sergeant, Leib-Bataillon, 1815

Other ranks wear the 1809 infantry shako with a drooping horsehair plume, black cockade, white loop and button, silver death's-head badge, and black bosses and chin-scales. The body of the shako is black felt, the top and headband leather. The coat is of the dolman style worn in Spain, with light-blue facings on collar and shoulder-straps; the black trousers had a light-blue side-stripe.

Silver rank chevrons were worn by N.C.O.s on the right upper arm, in the following sequence – corporal: two stripes; sergeant: three stripes; colour-sergeant: three stripes and a crown; sergeant-major: four stripes and a crown. All N.C.O.s carried a sabre in a black sheath, with a yellow and light-blue knot. Sergeants and above wore white gloves, and a yellow waist-sash with a blue central stripe, blue runners and whip tassels; while privates wore two black cross-belts supporting a plain black cartridge pouch and bayonet scabbard, and N.C.O.s wore a smaller pouch, centrally on the front of a narrow waist-belt worn over the sash.

D2 Trooper, Hussar Regiment in English service, 1809–15

The uniform of the hussars in British service differs little from that worn in the 1809 campaign. The waist-sash is now light-blue and crimson, and the black bandolier has no picker equipment. Instead of overalls the troopers wear black hussar breeches tucked into hussar boots decorated with a black tassel. A black pelisse is worn; it has a black fur edge, three rows of black buttons, and fourteen rows of black lace. N.C.O.s wore silver chevrons on the upper right arm; trumpeters wore troopers' uniform with silver and light-blue 'swallows' nests'.

Officer (left) and gunner, Artillery Regiment, 1815

D3 Captain, Hussar Regiment in English service, 1809–15

The shako now has a wide gold lace edging around the top, but is otherwise unchanged. The dolman is black with light-blue cuffs and collar decorated with black lace. There are five rows of buttons and fourteen rows of black lace on the chest, and black lace embroidery on the rear seams of the dolman. Black Hungarian knots are embroidered over the cuffs. The pelisse is like the dolman, but with black fur trim. Black breeches are embroidered with Hungarian knots on the thighs; they are tucked into hussar boots with gold top trim and tassels. The black bandolier has gold picker equipment and shield with *GR* cipher; sabre, sabretache and gloves are as in 1809, and a gold and crimson waist-sash and sabre-knot have been added. Horse furniture was as in 1809.

E1 Officer, Infantry Regiment in English service, 1809–15

The shako is as for the 1809 campaign. The hussar-style dolman, which has no skirts, has fourteen rows of black lace and five rows of buttons on the chest, black cuffs and a light-blue collar with black embroidery. The marks of rank are the crimson silk waist-sash in the hussar style, and a gold and crimson sword-knot. The black overalls have a light-blue side-stripe. A hussar sabre is carried in a steel sheath on black slings, as in the 1809 campaign.

E2 Officer, Leib-Bataillon, 1815

Very similar to that of other ranks, the officers' uniform is immediately distinguishable by the lack of equipment, and by the yellow and silver waist-sash. The knot of the cavalry-pattern sabre, with the usual furniture, is the same colour. The black dolman has five rows of buttons, and fine black embroidered decoration at cuffs, collar and rear seams. Majors and above, silver knots above the cuff, a black bandolier with silver picker equipment, and a black cartouche with a silver *FW* cipher on the flap.

Gelernte Jägers and (right) sergeant of the Leib-Bataillon, 1815

E3 Sharpshooter, Infantry Regiment in English service, 1809–15

The shako is the usual infantry other ranks' pattern. The dark-green tunic has a light-blue collar and light-blue Polish cuffs, very short light-blue turnbacks and a single row of yellow buttons. The light-grey trousers, worn over short black gaiters, have a narrow light-blue side piping. Equipment is the same as for privates of infantry, except for the British Baker rifle and sword-bayonet.

Officers of Sharpshooters are distinguished from those of the infantry only by the use of dark-green cloth instead of black for the dolman, and grey overalls in place of black.

F1 Sergeant-Major, 2nd Light Battalion, 1815

The rank badges, weapons, gloves and equipment of N.C.O.s of both line and light battalions follow exactly those described in *D1*. Shako decorations follow those of privates of the relevant battalion.

F2 Private, 3rd Light Battalion, 1815

There were few differences between the uniforms of the line and light battalions. The plate on the shako is a silver hunting horn depending from a round disc bearing the battalion number; and the light battlions' shako pompon is yellow over light-blue. The facing sequence of the three battalions was 1st Light Battalion: buff (until 1 July 1815, then rose-red); 2nd Light Battalion: yellow; 3rd Light Battalion: orange.

F3 Private, 2nd Line Battalion, 1815

The shako is as for the Leib-Bataillon, but has a plate in the form of a near semicircle under a disc bearing the battalion number. The plate bears the horse of Saxony with the motto *Nunquam Retrorsum*. In place of a plume, this soldier wears the pompon of the line battalions, about 4 in. high and equally divided light-blue over yellow. The circular black leather cockade is partly hidden by the numbered disc. The chin-strap is black leather. The waist-length tunic has no skirts, and bears battalion facings on the collar and shoulder-straps only. (The sequence was 1st Line Battalion: red; 2nd Line Battalion: green; 3rd Line Battalion: white.) The tunic has a single row of ten round black

**Officer,
infantry regiment**

G3 Drummer, 1st Line Battalion, 1815

The drummer wears the conventional shako. Drum slings and aprons are black, the former having an oval steel plate to hold the black drumsticks, which have steel ends. The drums have brass bodies, light-blue and yellow striped hoops, white tensioning cords and black carrying straps.

H1 Drum Major, 2nd Line Battalion, 1815

Shako decorations are conventional. The dolman has ten tasselled rows of lace, battalion facings on collar, shoulder-straps and 'swallows' nests', and silver decorations; silver lace knots are embroidered on the thighs.

H2 Officer, Horse Artillery Battery, 1815

Horse artillery officers dress exactly as officers of hussars, except that they wear black collars and Polish cuffs edged with gold lace and embroidery, and have yellow side-stripes on their trousers. (Note that in 1815 hussar officers also had black cuffs on the dolman.) Their men wear black dolman-style jackets with black collars and cuffs outlined in yellow, black buttons, lace and tassels. Black hussar-style overalls have a yellow side-stripe, and rank badges are as for the infantry but in yellow or gold. The shako is of hussar pattern with a white metal death's-head and a gilt grenade on the front, under a round black leather

glass buttons, and ten rows of doubled round black lace across the chest, with small tassels at each end. False pockets under each arm are outlined in lace, which also decorates the back of the tunic, and outlines the pointed black cuffs. The trousers have a side-stripe in the facing colour. Personal equipment is as in the Leib-Bataillon.

G1 Senior Musician, 1st Line Battalion, 1815

This musician wears the shako, like the privates of his battalion; but note that this plate shows the Russian *Kiwer* type.[8] 'Swallows' nests' are in black and the facing colour; or, for senior grades, gold with fringes and the facing colour (for the Leib-Bataillon, light-blue). He carries no musket, bayonet, cartridge pouch or pouch cross-belt – only a sabre in a black sheath, with a yellow and blue sabre-knot.

G2 Junior Officer, 2nd Line Battalion, 1815

Officers of both line and light battalions wear shako plates like those of the men of their battalion. They are distinguished by a 4 in. cut-feather plume, equally divided between yellow and light-blue in the sequence described above. Gloves were green in the light battalions, white in the line. Otherwise, uniforms, equipment and weapons follow those of the Leib-Bataillon, described in E2.

**Officer,
hussar regiment**

(Left) private, hussar regiment; (centre) private, light infantry regiment; (right) private, rifle company

cloth with black collars and cuffs edged in yellow and overalls in the same shade with black leathe inserts and yellow side-stripes. Horse artiller train drivers wear hussar-pattern shakos of th Russian *Kiwer* model, but with a yellow grenad badge in place of the death's-head. The black tunic has black collar, cuffs and turnbacks, all edged with yellow. There is a yellow braid collar decoration and yellow grenades in the four corners of the turnbacks, black braid decoration on the rear seams of the jacket, and black braid shoulder-straps. Black overalls with yellow side-stripes are worn; a black bandolier and pouch has yellow fittings and a yellow grenade badge. A brass-hilted sabre in a steel sheath has black leather slings and fist-strap.

cockade surmounted by a drooping black horse-hair plume.

Foot artillery officers wear the same uniform with a gilt grenade shako badge alone, and a short yellow cut-feather plume. Officers of the rank of major and above wear a bandolier and pouch. No spurs are worn. Foot artillery other ranks wear the hussar-pattern shako with a brass grenade badge replacing the death's-head, and a yellow pear-shaped pompon, about 4 in. high, replacing the plume. They wear infantry-cut tunics and infantry trousers over black gaiters and shoes, but all other distinctions are as for horse artillery rankers. Equipment includes brass-hilted sabres in black sheaths on a black bandolier for the foot, and hussar-pattern sabres on black slings for the horse artillery.

H3 Driver, Train of Foot Artillery, 1815
Drivers of the foot artillery train wear foot artillery shakos, tunics of infantry cut in a dark brown-grey

Napoleon (National Army Museum)

INDEX

Figures in **bold** refer to illustrations.